David Days

Thanks for all the support,

Your friend, David Days

Astrid's Origins: Academy Years

by David Days

Astrid's Origins
Academy Years

Introduction

-Astrid is a girl with a sparkling personality. Her parents had only her and that was more than enough. She's sweet and kind and she will be sooner or later the owner of a multi-million dollar company which is the principal benefactor of this academy... think about that-
-Did you seriously write that on your admission essay?- said Cody amazed at Astrid's boldness.
-Of course, and the greatest part is I got in!-
-YES! It will be amazing to be in the same school again- Cody said hugging her tight.

Cody and Astrid celebrated at the Academy's cafeteria when Randall passed by with his group of friends... he looked at her silently as he walked by. One of the guys who followed him whistled at her and Randall punched him in the stomach, he then winked at her and continued his path.

-Who... is... that?- she said drooling on Cody's arm.
-Oh no, that's Randall Omalley, his dad is Bob Omalley, but he's bad news, he's the Academy's biggest bully, he runs this place, he has been with

basically every girl in the whole academy- Cody said a little nervous.

-Not every girl- said Mickie jumping from behind Cody. He got surprised and kissed her.

-Ew, you two can get a room- Astrid said happy but disgusted at the same time. Her best decision was to fix them up together.

-I'm sorry kid, but I love this woman-

-How come I'm a kid and she's a woman? We're the same age!- Astrid said annoyed.

-Well I have my reasons to say it- Cody said with a sm le while looking deep into Mickie's eyes. Astrid puked in her mouth a little, they were all kids, and she knew he wasn't talking about sex, but it damn felt like it.

-Cody, stop traumatizing her, what were you guys talking about?- said Mickie escaping Cody's embrace and sitting next to Astrid.

-Well, first of all... I GOT ACCEPTED!!!-

-AHHHHH!!!!- Mickie yelled and hugged Astrid, they were both so excited. -ME TOO!!!!!-

-Ok, ok, there are some things you need to know about this place, first, you need to pick a brand color and dye your uniform with it, mine as you could see is yellow- he said showing his sleeve's border. -But be careful, if you choose a brand someone else already has you'd be paired up the

whole year-
-PINK!!!!- yelled Astrid. -OMG I'm soooo pink, but
dark pink, like a girly bad ass!- she said high fiving
Mickie.
-Well... I'll be purple, because is sorta like pink, but
it's not the same, so I won't be FORCED to pair with
you, I want to pair with you by my own choice-
Astrid seemed worried.
-But Mickie, what if someone else picks purple?!
At least if we're the same we can ask to be paired
up-
-Then change to purple-
-NO....CHANCE....IN...HELL that's happening-
-Ok, then we'll have to see what happens- Mickie
said with an evil expression.
-You know what happens, I kinda own this place,
and they'll do as I say, and you're my team for life!-
Astrid hugged Mickie and Cody joined them, now
they would all go to the same school again... but as
high schoolers.

The bells rang, Cody had to go to class, he quickly
kissed Mickie as he ruffled Astrid's hair, and ran
back into the Academy.

-Would you imagine actually coming to study in
here?- said Astrid with a sparkle in her eyes.
-That would be amazing, specially with all the guys-

Mickie said with a fresh smirk, elbowing Astrid.

-You're supposed to be my best friend's girl, so shhh-

-Yes, but I'm also your best friend- Mickie threw her arm around Astrid's shoulders. -So listen carefully, there is a guy here, Cody always talks about him, I've only seen him once, but he didn't even notice me, so dark, so cool-

-Randall?-

-OMG YES! Have you seen him?- Mickie couldn't help but drool.

-Yes I did- Astrid blushed. -Some guy whistled at me and he punched him- she said embarrassed.

-HE LIKES YOU!- Mickie said jumping.

-You're crazy, plus, I won't waste the opportunity to study in a place like this just to meet guys- Astrid said very decided.

-Oh no, don't tell me you're still obsessed with that guy- Mickie rolled her eyes.

A car parked as they were chatting at the entrance. Mickie's dad came to pick her up. He offered Astrid a ride as a guy in a motorcycle spinned his way inside.

- It's ok Mickie, my ride is here- she said with dreamy eyes. The guy took off his helmet, it was Mike Arlington, 10 years older, hot, wearing his sunglasses and his black and gold leather jacket.

4

-Good morning Mr. Jameson- he said waving at Mickie's disgusted father as Mickie stared, pressed against the window. -And good morning to you, princess- he winked at Mickie and she sat back fulfilled. Astrid jumped on the back of his bike and wore his spare helmet and they headed home.

-DADDY- Astrid jumped from the bike and ran to hug her dad... still wearing the helmet.
-Princess! How many times do I have to tell you not to mix with the likes of Mike Arlington?! It's dangerous for a twelve-year-old to be riding on the back of a motorcycle with a 22-year-old- he said with a menacing look to Mike. Mike shrugged and went inside the house.

Astrid at the time was living with her father and her uncle, while her mother studied in France, although Astrid's uncle, Shane, insisted that his sister just wanted to escape her insufferable husband. And Astrid's dad, Paul, said she wanted to go somewhere her leech of a brother wouldn't bother her. Either way, Astrid had her two favorite people in the world taking care of her, and her uncle's best friend, Mike, as personal chauffeur.

-How's my favorite niece ever?!- Shane picked her up on a hug. He's just ten years older than her, but he loves to make her feel smaller.

-I'm good, I got accepted into the Academy uncle Shane!-

-Why wouldn't you? Daddy practically owns most of the Academy, and they prepare you there to work in our company, so obviously you had to go there- Shane said taking away her victory and flipping some pancakes. -Have you picked a brand yet?- he said excited.

-I'm gonna be pink!... but daaaark pink- she said looking so cool. Shane and Paul looked at each other and shared a smile and a tear. -What's wrong people?-

-Nothing, your mom was dark pink branded too- Mike said taking off his jacket.

-BTW, what were you doing there so early? Classes don't start until tomorrow for new students- Shane said wiping his eyes.

-Oh, guess what, she wanted to have breakfast with the Runnelli and his girlfriend Jameson- Mike said as he threw himself on the couch.

-Princess! How many times do I have to tell you not to mix with the likes of Cody Runnelli?!- Shane said imitating Paul, with a finger under his nose like a mustache, which Astrid and Mike found hilarious... Paul not so much.

-Astrid, go upstairs, I need to teach your uncle some respect, I feel I got left in charge of two kids

instead of one- Paul said angrily. -... well three-
Paul turned to see Mike passed out on the couch,
he lowered his head in disappointment and sighed.
Astrid ran to her room, soon she heard knocks on
her window... It was Cody.

Cody had fled the Academy and went to kidnap
Astrid. Little did he know, Astrid was more than
ready to escape with him anywhere.

-Shouldn't we tell your dad?-
-No! Let's get Mickie!- Astrid said. Mickie got out
from behind some bushes.
-What do you mean, I picked her up first, it was her
idea to get you... oh, there is one more person I
want to invite-

Cody, Mickie and Astrid took the bus to the woods
(that's what they called the further place in town)
to the Hartford house.

-What are we doing at the Hartford house?-
Astrid said nervously, she had heard stories that
strange things happened in there.
-We came for him- Cody whispered as they hid in
the bushes.

Randall was at the door. He knocked and a guy his

age answered the door, they fist bumped and he was invited inside.

-We came for Randall?!- Mickie said fixing up her hair. Cody squinted at her.
-No… we came for HIM…- the door opened and a kid their age was kicked out, he seemed sad, depressed to say the least. Cody carefully got out from behind the bush and approached him. -Hi Jeffrey- he said offering his hand to help him stand up.
-Hi Cody, sorry you and your friends had to see that- Jeff said waving at the girls in the bush. Mickie and Astrid came out and introduced themselves.

Matt Hartford was Randall's best friend, and his little brother Jeffrey was just accepted into the academy. He was a quiet little boy, extremely well-behaved for his age… but the way Cody saw it, he was the perfect way into Randall's circle. Cody took his little gang to the ice cream parlor in the park. Astrid loves ice cream, and Cody and Mickie love to make-out, Jeff on the other hand, was a little uncomfortable watching.

-Don't look at them, talk to me, do you like your ice cream?-

-Sure, my dad doesn't let us eat sweets, so I don't have much to compare it too, it's good I guess-
-GOOD?! Ice creams are the best!, the only thing better than ice cream are Skittles-
-Squirthles?- said Jeffrey confused. Astrid couldn't believe her ears. She got some Skittles from the cashier and dumped a small amount on Jeffrey's hand, she saw him pick one and smell it.
-NO! Eat them all...- she said pushing his hand against his face. His eyes lit, his pupils dilated, like he just had cocaine mix with meth melted on an aluminum spoon and injected directly to his heart. He was so happy! So happy he felt embarrassed to be seen like that, so he stood up and left. Cody felt like something was missing and stopped kissing Mickie for a second, just to find out Jeffrey was gone.

-ASTRID MICHELLE! WHAT DID YOU DO??!!-
-You would have known if you weren't always so busy sucking Mickie's face! I honestly don't know why did you bring us here! I'm leaving too!- Astrid stood up and left.
-It was Mickie's idea!- Cody yelled. He wanted to resume his make out session, but Mickie pushed him away and ran after Astrid.
-I'm sorry Asti, Cody can sometimes be kinda clingy-

-Kinda is an understatement... but anyways it wasn't his fault that Jeff left, it was mine, he told me his father never let them taste sweets and I gave him Skittles-

-ASTRID MICHELLE! WHY?!- she said imitating Cody. Astrid and Mickie laughed and walked home.

-Hi Mr. Arlington- Mickie said flirtatiously to Mike as they walked through the door.

-Well hello princess, but you can call me Mike, Mr. Arlington is my father- Mike said holding her chin close to his face taking Mickie's breath away.

-Mike, don't you have a brother Astrid's age?- Shane said picking Astrid up and sitting her on his shoulders.

-Yes, but he lives with my mom in California, Dad would love for him to move in with us and to go to the Academy, but mom wants him as far away from my dad as possible, she says he would influence the boy's career choices... she wants him to be a cook- Mike took an apron as he said it.

-Why? is he gay like you?- the girls laughed with Shane's words, but Mike didn't find it funny.

-Ha! I know you wish I was gay, and even if I were, you're not my type, plus a man who cooks is not gay, it's sexy, right girls?- Mike looked at the girls with his apron on, pointing at them with a wooden spoon,

both girls blushed and nodded with a big smile.
-Umm, Astrid, Mickie, to the room! This got too creepy too fast- said an uncomfortable Shane shushing the girls away.

Mickie and Astrid went up to Astrid's room. They fixed up each other's hair and played dolls, reenacting the day they just had and everything they would have done differently. Mickie would've left her dad and jumped in on Mike's bike. Astrid never would have given Jeff Skittles, never would have yelled at her best friend. Mickie would have kissed Mike when their faces were that close. You could hear her laughs a mile away, but Mickie's father came for her. Tomorrow was their first day at the Academy.

First Day of School

Astrid got up really early, she couldn't wait to start classes at the Academy. She had a legacy to protect, her mom, her uncle, her godfather, her grandfather, they all went to the Academy and excelled on it, plus if she wanted to take care of the family business, she had to learn everything she could about it in class.

She started off great, she walked the big doors holding hands with Mike Arlington, another Academy legend. Back in his days, Mike and Shane used to run the school the way Randall and Matt run it now. When inside, Mike kissed her on the forehead and left her as she ran to Mickie in the lobby. Matt had just arrived with Randall and little Jeffrey. Randall shushed the kid away and strutted inside with his bro.

-Hi- said an embarrassed Jeffrey approaching Mickie while he looked at Astrid weird.
-Hi Jeff! Aren't you exci.... OMG MICKIE!!! LOOK!!!- Astrid yelled unable to hide her excitement, she pointed at Jeff's sleeve's borders.

Mickie tried to contain her and apologized to Jeffrey for what happened the day before with her and Cody, she hadn't realized Jeff had branded himself purple... but he did.

-Hey... we're wearing the same brand, what does that mean?- Jeff said all innocent, Mickie blushed and looked at Astrid, who shrugged with a smile.

-It means we're a couple-

-A COUPLE?!- he said all nervous and sweaty looking at both of them.

-No, no, we're coupled... paired, for class assignments, either way I'm studying with Astrid, so it mean the three of us are paired.

-It's ok, I would love to work with you... and Astrid-

-Oh, BTW, sorry about me and Cody yesterday-

-Don't worry, I didn't mind, Matt and Randall bring all kinds of dates to our house, I'm used to it... the thing is Astrid gave me candy and my father doesn't allow it, and I want to make my father proud- he said kinda angry at Astrid, but he sucked it up quick and calmed down.

-Oh! My crew is heeeereee!- yelled Cody as he ran towards them, kissed Mickie while he ruffled Astrid's hair. -And sure enough the newest addition to the pack! Aoooooooo!- he said as he hugged Jeffrey and howled.

-Wow, how are you not best friends with Randall and Matt?- said Jeffrey uncomfortably trying to free himself from Cody's hug.

-Because he is MY best friend and I won't share him with someone like Randall-

-Were you calling me?- Randall stood behind Astrid and she froze, but bravery runs in her family. She slowly turned around and faced him.

-Well hi, I wasn't calling you, I was talking about you... which is different... mainly because you weren't supposed to listen- Astrid stood even closer to Randall, his friends were taunting him, the little girl challenged him, and he wasn't one to turn down a challenge... but he half-smiled and turned around and left.

-Then keep talking, gorgeous!- he said as he walked away. Astrid's friends were in awe... just like the whole academy.

-The day came when a girl forced Randall's hand and won!- Cody shouted and everyone picked Astrid up in celebration.

-And he called you gorgeous! He likes you!- Mickie said almost crying. The principal came out because of the noise and everyone was sent to their classes.

But Astrid wasn't happy, she lost her brother Drew when she was only five years old, two years later her best friend John was taken away too, gladly she met Cody short after, but with John also left the love of her life, Mike McCoy, and she was sure she would never love again. It was kiddie childish love, a four year relationship which started when they were three years old, but for her it was true. Now she was everyone's hero because she had the biggest bully wrapped around her finger... but no pressure.

-It's just how I imagined! We can have lunch together everyday, I already have a new friend, I'm the queen of this place! People love me- Astrid said to her gang at lunch.
-Hi, Miss Callaway, Randall was wondering if you would like to sit with the seniors in their table- said one of Randall's minions sent to lure Astrid to their table. Astrid looked at Cody and Mickie who insistently nodded, but Jeff seemed unhappy... indifferent.
-That is very kind of Randy, but tell him I eat with my friends, if he wants me at the senior's table, we ALL go to the senior's table- Jeff lifted his head and smiled, exactly what Astrid wanted. Randall received the news and walked towards their table.
-Ok kid, you're new around here, so I will tell you how this works- he said surrounded by his followers and Matt. -I run this place, we're the popular side, if we invite you to be with us... it's just you- he said getting closer again.
-Well, the way I see it, you only have two years left

of reign- she pinched his cheek. -And then MY best friend Cody will run this place- she said pointing at Cody who hid under the table. -Well, when he leaves, we're gonna be the ones in charge, we even have a younger better looking Hartford to fill Matt's place- she said throwing her arm over Jeffrey's shoulders, he just lowered his head again. Randall and his guys laughed at her and left.

-Are you out of your mind?! He might not do anything to you, but he will kill us- Cody said kinda scared.
-Yes, I'm done as soon as I get home!- said Jeffrey with his hands on the head.
-Don't you see she was trying to protect you? She tried to earn you a place in the cool guys' table... it's her first day, maybe that's why that hottie Randall let you all live- Mickie said.
-Hottie, huh?- Cody was squinting at Mickie.
-Is that all you heard?!-
-Yes, but I can't be mad at Astrid- Cody turned and looked Astrid in the eyes. -I will never be mad at you- they hugged... but Jeffrey was still worried for his life.

The bell rang as the first day of school came to an end. Mike came to pick Astrid in his sweet Motorcycle. Cody's half brother Goldo was sent to

17

pick up Cody but offered Mickie a ride as well, and Jeff waited outside for his brother Matt.

-What's up with that girl, dude? She's cute, but you can'- lose credibility just to please her- said Matt as he walked out with Randall.
-I know, but there is something in her, you know, she's not like all the dumb girls we juggle-
-You mean... you liiiike her- Matt started punching Randall in the stomach playfully.
-I'm not saying I do, but if I did, I guess this would be how it feels, no?- Randall said a little embarrassed. They both saw Jeffrey sitting on the side walk and approached him, Jeffrey saw them and tried to pray his way into heaven, but Randall just offered him his hand. -So you're the one who is going to replace Matt, huh?-
-No... I...- Jeff was really nervous and scared. But Matt squatted a little and ruffled his hair.
-I wouldn't like it any other way, little brother- Jeff calmed down and smiled. They all got into Randy's car and drove home.

-So tell me about your new friend, Jeffrey- Randall said throwing his backpack in their living-room couch.
-Her name is Astrid Callaway, but she's a Brooks too, I guess that is why she got in. She's very

interested in taking over the business, but really wants to be a model... honestly I'm relieved, I wouldn't want to end up working for her-

-So you want to work there too?!- Randall said surprised and looked at Matt who shrugged and handed him a root beer.

-Anyone who wants to be successful in that business need the proper education, and the Academy brings just that!- Jeffrey said with conviction.

-Mr. Hartford, good evening, I didn't know you were here- Randy said nervous as he stood up when Matt and Jeff's dad walked down the stairs.

-Relax Randall, I know Matt is the bad influence here, keep drinking, I'm just proud that my little precious rainbow is not as weak as you- he said hugging Jeffrey. -How was your first day at school with your brother?-

-I made new friends papa, with influential families in the business-

-Ha ha ha, that's all you think about, and do I know any of these "Influential families"?- Jeffrey's dad said proudly.

-You must, Brooks, Jameson and Runnelli- Jeffrey's dad was surprised.

-I was really good friends with the Jamesons back in the day, you know?-

-REALLY?!- Jeffrey's eyes sparkled, but soon he

realized his father had said "was". -What do you mean was? What happened?-

-Nothing, when your mother died we got overwhelmed by debt, so I was forced to lower our way of living, we moved to a more affordable place and kept the money for the important things, like your education, but my high class friends didn't understand that... you know who really helped me a lot? Paul Callaway, he's a great man-

-THAT'S MY FRIEND'S DAD!!- Jeff said excited. And his father cried a little.

-I somehow knew that my boy would be friends with them, I pushed him away because I didn't want to hold him back, and I heard he married rich-

-Yes, he married a Brooks, to say the least, smart guy- Matt said while clinging his beer with Randall's.

-Don't be disrespectful Matthew, I'm talking to your brother, why don't you go be irresponsible somewhere else?- Matt felt bad for being scolded in front of his friend, but Randall was used to it, they took their jackets, Randall took his backpack and they left.

-Papa, you shouldn't be so hard on him-

-I want him to understand he needs to grow up, my boy- he kissed Jeffrey's forehead and stood up. -I have to make a trip... it's a work thing, if this deal

I'm making turns out the way I planned, we will have tons of money to buy you that pool you always wanted!-

-But papa, I'm ok playing with the hose, as long as you're here to play with me- Jeffrey's dad hugged him crying.

-But you deserve a pool, and a mansion, and cool clothes, and I want to give that to you- Jeffrey didn't understand why his dad cried, but he hugged him tight and then went to do his homework.

Connections, Connections, Connections!

Astrid got home to another fight between her father and her uncle Shane, Mike was sitting in the living-room reading a book when she jumped on top of him and snuggled with him.

-Why do they always have to fight, Mike?-
-Because your father sucks, he killed our best friend and he'll never admit it- Astrid looked at him angry. -That's not a discussion for you princess, tell me about your first day- he said stroking her hair.
-Well, I stood up to a bully to defend my friends, I don't know if it worked, but hey, I didn't die- Mike was surprised.
-Kudos to you! I didn't know you cared that deeply about your friends, that's sweet-
-I also made a new friend, he's amazing, a little shy though, his name is Jeff Hartford- Mike looked at her as if she was kidding, but when he realized she wasn't, he got serious.
-You can't befriend a Hartford, Astrid, its too dangerous, I knew you should've waited another year-

-No! He's great, his brother on the other hand is besties with the bully I faced-
-Wait a second, you stood up to Randall Omalley?! Are you out of your mind?!-
-Why?!- Astrid was starting to get scared.
-The Hartfords are criminals, they only hurt those around them, didn't you know they stole a lot from YOUR OWN family, your father, who helped them get back on their feet, I don't want you to have friends like that... I forbid you even! And don't let me get started on what Randall will do to you... better what I'll do to him if he touches you with his filthy womanizer hands-
-You can't blame a little kid for his father's mistakes! And if you do, why would you even talk to me if you say my father is a murderer?! You can't forbid me anything, you're not my father, nor my tutor, nor my boyfriend, you're just my uncle's leech, and I hate you!-

Astrid ran to her room crying, Paul and Shane got to see half of the fight, but her yelling was heard in the whole block, Paul sat with Mike to hear his version of the story first.

-Paul, I'm sorry, I was just trying to protect her, you know what the Hartfords did to you-
-It was one Hartford and yes, he was supposed to be

my friend, but I forgave him a long time ago, doesn't mean his son will be like him. And remember her circle is the Runnellis and the Jamesons, and if the Jamesons accept the Hartford kid, then we have nothing to worry about-
-I think I should go apologize then- Mike said regretful.

He went up to Astrid's room, she was crying on her bed, her notebook opened... she tried to do her homework, but was hard enough with the tears. Mike sat next to her and stroke her hair.

-I'm sorry princess, I was out of line, I know I'm not a direct part of this family, but you know you guys are family to me, and you're all the family I got. My parents are too busy with my baby brothers to pay attention to me, but Shane treats me like a true brother-
-My mom used to say you two were siamese twins born apart- Astrid chuckled and wiped her tears. Mike hugged her and kissed her head.
-And you are my favorite niece, I don't want anything bad to happen to you, I will kill them all if they hurt you-

Astrid was happy again, her platonic love for Mike grew stronger every day. Weeks passed and school was going great. Jeffrey was the first of the class, best grades, best attendance record, he was the star. Astrid's group was sitting at the popular kid's table, and they were under Randall's protection, everything was going well... maybe too well.

-Hello little one- Randall said as he cornered Astrid at the exit.
-Hello Randy, I think you're too close-
-It is Randall, and you didn't seem to care when you were facing me all brave-
-Well I like Randy better, it's cute, shows humanity, Randall sounds like the evil lizard from Monsters Inc.- Randall chuckled and stepped aside.
-Well Randy it is. I like your fire, aren't you even a little bit scared?-
-Oh, I'm terrified, but my mother always told me that we are the bravest when we're shitting our pants- Astrid was nervous, but she had to laugh, Randy laughed too, he got closer to her face with the intention of kissing her... but Mike showed up and pushed Randy.

-No! No no no! Astrid Michelle, you're coming with me!- Mike said furious.
-I can take you in my car, it is safer than this old man's bike- Randy said dusting his jacket off. Mike got even angrier and didn't let Astrid answer, he

took her by the arm and dragged her to the bike and left.

Mickie was chatting with Jeffrey at the exit when Matt approached them.

-Hi little brother- he said leaning over Jeffrey. -So this is one of your new friends, the Jameson girl, have you been to her house yet? It's amazing- Matt knew what he was doing, but Jeffrey was not going to let him.
-No, I haven't, we hang out at Cody's house mostly, and twice at Astrid's- Jeffrey said very natural, but it didn't work as he planned.
-You're right, you don't know my house, you don't even know my dad, we should have a sleepover at the Jameson household, ha ha ha-

Mickie's dad just arrived and she gave Jeffrey a kiss on the cheek and waved at Matt, leaving without an opportunity for Jeffrey to answer... he was doomed, if she knew that their fathers didn't like each other... it was over. Mickie was Astrid's bestie, and Astrid would choose her, and she was Cody's girlfriend and he would definitely pick her. All lost over a stupid brotherly bother!

-WHY?!- Jeffrey lost control, he jumped his

brother, he kicked him, punched him, spit on him, but Matt couldn't stop laughing, Jeffrey cried a great deal until Randy came out and carried him off Matt.

-I see you are enjoying brotherly time, I'm getting jealous- Randall chuckled.

-Sure? Don't lie, I know Selena punched you around from time to time- Randy got angry, dropped Jeff and kicked Matt a little.

-You never mention Selena again, ok?-

-Why? She's so hot, just mentioning her makes me.....oooh, even more if I picture her beating you up-

Randy didn't want to hurt his only friend, he can be a bully, but one with love in his heart, at least for his ONLY true friend. He left Matt and got into his car, he wanted to leave, but he waited for Matt and Jeffrey to get in and gave them a ride to their house. Randy lived in a loving home with his parents, he has a younger brother who lived in Missouri with his grandpa and his older sister who traveled a lot was staying with them, but she was... a mighty shadow to be covered by. She was the star of the house, winning every pageant she was on, tough as a tree, in a way Astrid reminded him of her.

-Hi mommy- Randy said walking through the door.
-MY BEAUTIFUL BOY!- Randy's mom hugged him and checked on him from head to toe. -Aw, Randall, you look homeless, I told you if you are going to hang with the Hartfords, you don't have to dress like them, sigh, but tell me about school, please- she sat with him on a chair.
-Well, there's a girl...- Randy's mom jumped. She went to the kitchen and yelled.
-Bobby, come quick, there's a girl, there's finally a girl!- Randy started to feel embarrassed, he felt his mom thought he was gay for Matt Hartford. Randy's dad ran to where they were and sat next to him.
-So! A girl! Tell us all about it champ!-
-Yes... tell everything...- said Selena walking slowly towards him. She was a gorgeous woman, basically chiseled into perfection by a modeling god.
-It's no big deal, I think I like her, but I'm sure she doesn't like me, so it is fine-
-No it's not, you are the most handsome boy in that whole academy, she should be drooling over you, never the opposite- Selena said, to which Randy was happily surprised.
-Wow, thanks sis, but it's not gonna happen either way, there are rumors that she will leave the academy and study modeling overseas, she's preparing for some kind of pageant where the prize

is a full scholarship in France-

-Don't you worry your pretty little head baby brother, your big sister is on the case, I won't stop until you get that girl- she pinched his cheek which annoyed him and he left to his room.

-Awww, don't you love how they love each other? we should have another one- said Randy's mom, but Randy's dad got nervous and sweaty.

-We should wait for Randy to graduate at least- with that said he left for work.

Selena started plotting her wicked plan, the first step was to get Astrid to trust her.

Selena Omalley

Another common day at the Callaway-Brooks'.
Arguing is in the air, while Astrid lives in a bubble
of happiness where everyone gets along and Mike is
her boyfriend... until Selena appears.

-Someone answer that door!- Mike yelled from the
kitchen. Astrid ran downstairs to answer for him.
She opened the door and Selena was there, she
looked innocent and nice, surely not as the Viper
she really is.
-Hi, my name is Selena, sorry to bother you, but I'm
new in town and I was going door to door
introducing myself to my new neighbors-
-That is so sad, come in, please, look no further, you
have a friend in me, you don't need to meet anyone
else, I'll help you!- Astrid said with a big smile.
Selena knew Astrid wouldn't give up the
opportunity to look humble an nice in front of
Mike, or her friends, or herself, or the world.
-Thank you, you're very kind, but I don't want to
bother you-
-Nah, it's no bother, I'll call my friends right now
and I assure you'll love them and they you-

Astrid made a few phone calls and in a couple of minutes Jeffrey and Mickie were hanging out with Selera. Since she travels a lot she wasn't a lot at home, so no one outside of Randy's family had actually seen her... well, just Matt, but Randy forbid him from telling anyone. When Cody burst through the front door their eyes met, everything stopped, it was just them, Selena fell in love, but then Cody saw Mickie and ran to her. Selena was confused, she has always been the prettiest everywhere, what was going on?!

-Hi, I'm Selena- she said nervously shaking Cody's hand.
-Umm, hi, I'm Cody Runnelli, Yes, THOSE Runnellis- he said very proud and cocky, little did he know he was talking to an Omalley.
-I'm very glad to meet you all, your families all work at...-
-Yep! My family runs the whole company!- Astrid jumped in.
-That's so cool, I'm not actually into that, I'm a model, I moved here because of a pageant...-
-NO WAY! The petite princesse etoile pageant?! I wanted to go too!- Astrid jumped in again, little did she know Selena didn't know the name of the pageant and she just told her, because the Omalleys always land on their feet.

-The one with the scholarship, yes-

Astrid eyes sparkled, finally a friend out of the business to talk to about modeling, it was too good to be true, and so their friendship started. Selena rented a room in a house next to Astrid's, a humble one where they all could visit and hang out, they went out for ice cream every sunday, they called it "Selena's Sunday Sundaes". She became an important part of their gang, with the added bonus that she was having an affair with Cody, behind Mickie's back. Selena was not at the Academy with them, she was older, just graduated from a modeling prep school, so she would... harass... Cody at night, while he spent the whole daylight with Mickie, but Astrid was no fool.

-Are you banging my new friend, Cody?!- Astrid yelled banging the door at Cody's. Max, the butler, answered the door.
-Hi Miss Callaway, always a pleasure, I'll get Mr. Runnelli for you-
-Sorry Max... thanks- Astrid sat angry on their couch waiting for Cody. He ran down the stairs very happy to see her, but she jumped him and put her tiny hands around his throat.
-Wha... goi... o.... Ast...- he tried to talk but the words wouldn't go out of his crushed pipe... so he

tickled her, getting off her grasp. -Are you insane? What's wrong with you?!- he said checking his neck on a mirror.

-One word... Selena- she said still angry. Cody got really nervous. -Exactly the reaction I wanted to see, Cody, I love you, you're my best friend and you came into my life when I really needed you... but Mickie is my best friend too. If you want to be with Selena, just break up with her-

-I can't leave Mickie... I love her, I truly do- he said as if he was saying it for the first time out loud. -Mark my words, I will marry her and name our kid after you- Astrid was touched by Cody's words.

-Astrid won't do if it's a boy- she said with a smile and a soft punch.

-Well, if a boy, it will be Astor-

-That is such a cool name, now I wish I was a boy- they laughed and everything was good for a second. -I'm glad to hear you won't be seeing Selena again-

-Uhhh, I never said that, have you seen Selena?! She's got boobs!- Astrid was disgusted and started hitting him playfully.

-Cody, you're a pig, you have to decide, or I won't be your friend anymore, I have your back whatever... well, whoever you decide, but you have to decide-

Astrid stood up and left, leaving Cody with a difficult choice, to keep secretly banging the hot older woman while still having a girlfriend who is the love of his life, or choosing a side.

A month passed and Cody was MIA, he didn't return Astrid's calls, or Mickie's, or Selena's, or Jeffrey's, he wasn't receiving visits at home, and he walked in and out of his classes avoiding his friends.

-I have to confess something Astrid, it's all because of me- said Selena while visiting Astrid's house.
-Don't say that, I talked to him a month ago and told him a lot of hurtful things, I'm the problem, I guess I should get a boyfriend and leave him alone-
-Ugh, no, I swear it's me, nothing is going right for me lately, I tried to enter the pageant and they told me I lack an inch to qualify... AN INCH!-
-Hmmm, maybe you can do something for me and I can do something for you- Selena knew how to manipulate a girl like Astrid and she finally got it, Astrid would offer to help her get into the pageant if Selena helped her get a boyfriend.
-So a Quid pro Quo? I'm listening- Selena said hiding the excitement of victory.
-Hmm, I don't know what that means, but a favor for a favor, I know people organizing the pageant, I could see if I can get you in...iffff-

-Whatever you want, tell me-

-You could help me get a boyfriend-

-Is that all?! Consider it done! You're rich, gorgeous, funny and feisty, it's the easiest quest ever make it a challenge, is there any boy at school tough enough?- Selena said knowing the answer to that.

-Well, there's this guy, his name is Randy Omalley, he's the toughest guy in school, and he's fairly cute, it would be cool to be his girlfriend-

-Uff, done, give me his address-

-I don't think anyone knows where he lives-

-Nice, added difficulty, I'll find out. Tomorrow starts Operation Randy Pandy! I'll text you everything you have to do tomorrow and you give me a play by play of how he responds- Selena was definitely having fun setting a trap for Astrid, right in her face, but let's say Astrid was even since she told Cody to stop seeing her. Selena left and went to her parent's house to see her baby brother.

-It was easier than I thought- she said dropping herself gracefully on their living room couch.

-Easy, it only took you what... four months?- Randy said sitting next to her.

-Five actually, but I got it, tomorrow she will start flirting with you, I need you to show indifference-

-But I am... different... about it- Randy said

confused. Selena tried not to kill him and put her head on his lap.

-This is how it's going to go baby brother, I'm "helping her" get a "boyfriend", and you are that boy, so it would be suspicious if you jumped her as soon as she said hi, I guarantee satisfaction, just play by my rules- Selena seemed determined... but Randy was her brother, he could see right through her.

-What do you get out of this?-

-What do you mean?- she said sitting quickly.

-You are not doing this to help me, out of the goodness of your heart, you must be getting something in return-

-I'm critically offended! You're my only brother-

-What about Nate? "Your cutest brother" Yes, I heard you over the phone last night-

-Well, I mean, my only brother... in this town... close to me, you get it, and I know I haven't been there for you much, but I want your happiness above all things!- she dramatically pushed some tears and stormed out before Randy could even answer. He rolled his eyes and rested assure that her getting something or not, either way he was getting Astrid.

Someone's got a boyfriend!

The next day Astrid went to the Academy more nervous than ever, she said hi to Mickie, who was just getting in as well.

-Hi Mix, I guess it's just you and me now-

-I know, I can't believe Cody is avoiding us, what can be so hard that he couldn't share it with us?- Mickie said incredibly sad.

-I have no idea... on other news, have you seen Jeff? I didn't see him in the whole weekend-

-Oh, you didn't know? His father died, he was working overseas and Matt got notice that he died over there-

-How would you know that before I did! I'm his friend and his future employer, he used to tell me everything!-

-I just know everything- Mickie shrugged and Astrid looked at her with her arms crossed waiting for an explanation. -Well, I invited him to my house and he didn't show up, I went to his and Matt told me, he asked me to bring him the homework after school-

Astrid was shocked, her mom was overseas, she

knew what that was like, Jeffrey used to talk for hours about how his dad would come back and buy him a pool. After school she would definitely go over to Jeffrey's and help them out. Astrid was really sad, she sat for a moment and a tear ran through her cheek, but was stopped by Randy's finger.

-You shouldn't cry... so don't do it- Randy said uncomfortable. He had good intentions but wrongly placed.
-Thanks Randy, but my friend's dad died- she couldn't help it and hugged Randy tight and started crying. Randy hugged her and stroke her hair.
-I know, mine too- he said sad... although with the same expression. Matt was Randy's only true friend and he wasn't going to school either. Astrid's phone beeped, it was a message from Selena.

"First things first, you want to let him know you're in control, so never let him see you cry... you tend to do that a lot. Second, try to appear strong, I heard you stood up to him and he liked it, so keep it that way, zero weakness. And third for today, stop showing empathy, you have your crew, but they're not as important as you. Good luck. S"

-Well great- Astrid said wiping her tears and sitting defeated.

-Umm, what's great?- Randy said confused since she was crying a second ago.

-In all honesty which is how I work, I asked a girl to help me out getting you to be my boyfriend and I just failed horribly in the first three minutes of school- there was an awkward silence.

-Technically school hasn't started, if it did he would've gone to his classes and we were gone to ours- Mickie said trying to break the silence. Randy seemed embarrassed, he turned around and left without saying a word. Astrid realized what she said and blushed while Mickie just shook her head.

-You blew it-

-I was sad, I couldn't help it, I didn't actually NEEDED a boyfriend anyways-

-True, you have Mike... speaking of...-

-PRINCESS!!!- Astrid turned around and Mike was running towards her. -You left your lunch at home, I went to get it and back before classes started, it must be a new record- he said giving her a beat-up lunch bag with money inside. Astrid laughed. He kissed her forehead and walked away.

-He's not my boyfriend-

-He surely is not your not boyfriend- Mickie said elbowing her. Astrid threw back an evil smirk.

-Well, he's exactly what I need-

Randy was listening to them and was about to walk in to talk to her, but the bell rang. At lunch time everyone was at the cafeteria and Randy pulled Astrid aside.

-I wanted to tell you something- Randy was nervous and sweaty.
-OMG WHAT?!- Astrid had an idea, but as she yelled everyone looked at Randy. He got serious all of a sudden.
-I... I was wondering about your friend, ummm, the Runnelli, he's not sitting with us-
-Yeah, he's mad at me, nothing time won't heal, I believe in our friendship- Randy half-smiled and turned away.

When school was over, Randy approached Astrid... again, nervous... again, and tried to talk to her, but as soon as they were alone... they were not, Cody appeared and asked to steal Astrid for a second.

-I heard what you told Randall...-
-It's Randy now, we're calling him Randy-
-Don't interrupt me!- he said laughing and shaking her by the shoulders. -You're the best friend anyone could ask for, you made me see I was wrong. I do

love Mickie, and I won't do whatever I was doing anymore, I can't believe I'm saying this, but I'll tell Selena it's over-

-YOU WILL WHAT?!- Mickie overheard the conversation as she was leaving and went there furious.

-NOTHING!- Astrid yelled. -He is gonna tell Selena he won't be friends with her anymore!-

-Aha, and why is that?- Mickie said suspicious.

-Well because...- Astrid began to explain.

-I want Cody to say it-

-Well, the thing is Selena was making me choose between her and... Astrid... and I chose Astrid... from now on I will always choose Astrid- he said gazing into Astrid's eyes.

-Ehm!-

-Of course, except in love, umm marriage, baby making!-

-Cody, I think she got it- Astrid said stopping his embarrassment.

-I chose Astrid, and now I can't be friends with Selena- Astrid was lost in Cody's words. He's her best friend, she knows she means a lot to him, but his priority was always Mickie, it felt good to be chosen! When she came back into her senses she was wrapped around Cody's head and Mickie was furious about it. Mike came and without asking a thing he took Astrid and rode away.

It was late at night, everyone was asleep when Astrid heard knocks on her window. She thought it was Cody. She approached the window, opened it and a rock hit her in the head.

-Ouch.-

-Can I go upstairs?-

-What are you doing here?!- she said... to Randy as he climbed up her window.

-Cody told me this was the only true way to get you alone-

-Well, there are other ways... you could have asked, but what's done is done, What's up Randy?-

-I have never met someone like you, you're tough yet vulnerable, you're feisty yet sweet, you love and defend your friends but have no problem pushing them around, all things why I like you-

-Wait, you just said you like me!-

-Don't ruin it, please- Randy said with a smile. He got down on one knee. -Astrid, would you do me the honor of being my girlfriend?-

-YESS, YESS, YESS, YESSSSSS!- Astrid jumped everywhere waking up Shane and Paul.

-What's going on here??!!- they both said entering at the same time, they saw Randy knelt and Astrid jumping around him, Shane held him down as Paul was about to hit him with his sledgehammer.

-WAIT! NO! He's my boyfriend!-

-YOUR WHAT??!!- they looked at each other and Astrid shrugged, so they let him go.
-Well try to visit at normal hours!- Shane yelled as he jump through the same window he came from... landing on his feet... the Omalleys always land on their feet.

Somehow Selena kept her part of the bargain and now Astrid had to fulfill hers. The next day she called the board of the pageant very early and with some teeny tiny bribes she got Selena in. She went down to have breakfast with her family very proud of her life, but Shane threw it all out the window when he saw Mike come through the door.

-Somebody has a booooooyfrieeend- he said in a gossipy tone. Mike was surprised, and angry, and scared.
-Who does?!-
-Well, we're just three in here, sadly the jerk here is married to my sister, and you know if I played for that side you'd be the first to know so...-
-We're four Shane, she lives with three men, the fact that I don't sleep here doesn't take away my role in raising her- Mike said still confused and alarmed.
-Ok, first, I LIVE with two men, second, Neither you nor Shane is raising me... basically daddy is

raising the three of us, third, I'm the one who has a boyfriend, I wanna be clear, leave it out in the open, I'm dating Randy Omalley, yes, I know he is an Omalley, yes I don't care, and I hope you all be ok with that because it is my life, plus, I won't need Mike to take me to school, Randy has a car and he offered to pick me up-

-Hun, so there's a good side to all this, you won't be riding on that metal death horse again- Paul said stuffing his face with pancakes. Mike threw his helmet on the floor and stormed out.

-Paul, why would you say that? You ride a motorcycle while working!- said Shane angry.

-Yes, but inside the building and only on special events- he said with his mouth full.

-Nevermind, Should I go after him? it might not be safe- Shane said standing from the table.

-He'll be fine, he has a spare helmet on the bike- said Astrid as she stuffed her face with pancakes like her father.

Randy's car was outside he blew the horn once and Astrid was standing at his door. He got out and opened the door for her, as Paul and Shane stared intensely. She waved goodbye and they went to the Academy.

They walked through the door holding hands and

48

the whole Academy was dead silent, the bell rang and Randy gave her a soft kiss on the lips and went to his classes. As soon as he left, everyone surrounded her with a million questions "Is he sweet to you?" "Do you know where he lives?" "Have you met his parents?" "Does he look like his mom?" "Does he really live with the Hartfords?" "Is Matt part of your relationship?" "Does he smile?" "Is he capable of joy?" The questions were dumb and immature, so Astrid just pushed the people away and went to class. She received a letter from the chair behind, it came from Mickie, so they started old-school texting with notes.

"Is it true?"
"Yes, it's official"
"I'm happy for you, now we can go on double dates"
"I thought that's what we were doing with Jeff"
"BTW, I'm worried, where is him?"
"I heard he joined a gang after his father's death"
"I heard he was stealing to survive and he stopped coming here because he couldn't pay tuition anymore"
"I heard Matt had to eat him"
"Wow, that's dark, Tix"

-Ladies, is there anything you'd like to share with us?-

-No!- said both girls at the same time, but the paper fell and the teacher picked it up.
-Let's see- the teacher started reading. -Well, very interesting but I assured you Mr. Hartford haven't been eating by his brother, in fact the younger Hartford have been taking classes with yours truly at his house, and although I truly appreciate and encourage empathy and concern between classmates, I have to send the both of you to detention after school-

When school was over Mickie and Astrid had to spend three hours in detention. Cody and Randy met them at detention's door.
-Look at you, one day as my girlfriend and already on detention- Randy said pulling Astrid into a kiss.
-I have to admit I do find this rebel side of you really tempting- Cody said doing the same to look cool. But Mike showed up and pushed Randy away.

-I told you he was bad news, you've never been to detention in your life! One day as this kid's girl and look at you! You're coming with me, Paul would figure something out with the school board, we can't have you with a mark on your personal record- Mike took her by the arm but she wiggled her way out.
-No! I made a mistake which wasn't at all Randy's

fault, and I'm paying for the consequences, stop talking like you're my father or my uncle- Astrid took Mickie and strutted in the detention room and sat in the front row and used the time to do her homework. Both Mike and Randy waited for her outside and she picked Randy to take her home, which made Mike insane. Astrid was no longer his little princess, she grew up and was dating boys.

Months passed and the day of the pageant finally came. Astrid proudly had half of the audience on her feet. I mean, she brought Cody, Mickie, Mike, Shane, Paul, Randy, she even got Matt to go, she tried calling Jeffrey but he wouldn't pick up, but she left him a thousand messages. The pageant began and she saw Selena was on her group even though she was eight years older, she watch as every performance was being sabotaged except for Selena's and eventually there was only Selena and her. They hugged, wished each other good luck and then Selena betrayed her, made her trip, made fart noises when she was answering question and on the end she won... Selena won! She got the scholarship to study professional modeling in France.

-I'm so sorry, you lost, my dear friend, but the prettiest one won- Selena said all cocky.

-You'll never be prettier than me! You're just a cheater!-

-I'm not, I just have more experience in pageants- she shrugged. Astrid was furious, she wanted to jump her, but she had skipped physical education in school, so she was not in shape to fight an older woman, gladly Cody came with flowers.

-Thanks Cody, wasn't I great out there?- said a blushing Selena taking the flowers from Cody's hands.

-Sorry, but these are for Astrid- Cody said, snatching back the flowers and giving them to Astrid. -You were without a doubt the prettiest girl out there- Selena was furious and it was evident.

-No Cody... Selena won, she deserves the flowers- she said giving the flowers to Selena to which both Cody and Selena gasped surprised. -I got the best prize, she goes away and I stay with you- she said jumping into Cody's arms. Cody chuckled, everything made sense now. Selena's face got into different shades of red and she threw the flowers and stomped away.

-Are you really ok with her leaving?- Cody said while holding Astrid.

-Of course not, I wanted to get that scholarship, I don't needed, I could buy the whole school in France if I want to, but I wanted to prove I deserved it, plus my dad refuses to pay for a career in modeling, so I would have to wait until I was 21-said a sad, annoyed Astrid while still holding Cody's neck. He took her with the group and she stepped aside to talk to Randall.

Astrid was so angry she wanted to hit Selena in the face, and a thing which also threw her off during the competition was the way they called her "Miss Omalley" like how common can that last name be? She was furious, so she had to ask.

-Randy... do you know that girl? You share a last name-
-She could be a distant cousin, Omalley's are not common, but I don't know her- he said very natural. Astrid believed the lie and gladly she never had to see that bitch again.

The New and Improved
Jeffrey Hartford

Weeks passed and Matt came back to school... or so they thought. Randy saw him and he couldn't hide his happiness, he jumped Matt with a bro hug, but Matt pushed him away. Everyone was silent, Matt went to the Principal's office and stayed there a long while, Randy waited for him outside. When he got out he seemed disappointed, but at peace.

-Are you out of your mind?! I've missed you! Why would you push me away?- Randy said really worried, But Matt only looked at him for a second and kept walking. -Don't you love me anymore?- Randy said trying to stop him and kiss him.
-Randy, it's time you grow up, friend, I have, I need to take care of my family now, no time for childish immature games with you, get new friends if you can, I'm out-

Randy stood silent watching him go. Matt was his only true friend, and if it wasn't him it won't be another. From then on Randy wouldn't let anyone in, because having friends and caring for people only leads to humiliation and heartbreak.

But that was not the only surprise of the day. Astrid and Mickie went to class as soon as the bell rang, but there was someone already inside. No one used to beat them to the classroom... no one except...

-JEFFREY!- they both yelled as they approach the shadow, he turned around but it was different.
-What's up little bunnies- he said with a wink, he had died his hair red, yellow, blue, green and purple, all at the same time. He wore jeans to school, he had a piercing on an eyebrow, it was... weird, he changed his brand from purple to rainbow color... insane.
-Jeffrey, what did you do? When did you get here? What happened?-
-It's Jeff now ladies, just Jeff, and I came to class early, I broke a window and got in at 6am, then finished my nap in here, I would've come with Matt, but that party-pooper kept telling me to sit straight and to stop howling at girls on the street, so I jumped off the car-

Astrid and Mickie were astonished, the world turned upside down, Matt's rebelliousness got into Jeff's body as soon as it left Matt's. Either way, they had their friend back, and a more fun one it appears. The class started, and Jeff kept being the smartest, but now in a chill, cocky, unnerving way, he was... a cool nerd. Sooner than later came lunch time and they reunited with Cody. The girls put him up to date with everything Jeff related before Jeff showed up... but when he did, well everyone noticed.

-Hi guys, look what I found at home!- he said placing a gun on the table. Everyone alarmed and soon enough the Principal was there.
-Mr. Hartford, I understand what you're going through, but you can't bring weapons to this school-
-How would you know what I'm going through, fatty?- he said with a chuckle. -Your dad didn't die overseas, his dead is not your fault because you wanted something stupid like a pool, and of course your brother doesn't have to quit school because there's not enough money to live and keep both of us in school, so please man go away- everybody looked at him in shock, but he turned around as if nothing happened and kept talking to his friends. - Look guys, apparently it was my grandfather's, I saw on the internet this is how you cock it- he pulled the safe and cocked the gun, then he started fiddling with the trigger playfully, to which his

friends laughed, the principal started to worry.
-Mr. Hartford, please! Give me the gun, put it down!-
-Relax chief, I took the bullets out, I'm not an idiot, look!- he pointed at the Principal aimlessly and pulled the trigger... and shot the Principal's leg. Everyone started screaming and their friends stared at him. -Oops! I forgot the one on the chamber... oh well, I guess school's over for today, wanna go for ice cream?- he stood up and walked away.
-It's like he's a different person- Mickie said scared.
-Yes! I like it- yelled Astrid following him.
-I know, he's so cool- Cody said going with them. They all left and Randy met Astrid as she headed outside.

-Hey, umm, Astrid, can I go with you guys?-
-Sure! there's always room for one more in ice cream!-

They went out and Matt was outside, he leaned to talk to Jeff, they are just three years apart, but behaviorally it was like a father talking to a 5 year old.
-It's early to get out of school- Matt said with a smile knowing they were skipping class.

-Someone shot the principal, so while he gets to the doctor, the school is temporarily unsafe... so we're going for educational ice cream!-

-Did you shot the principal?- Matt said calmed but a little disappointed.

-I might have, with grandpa's gun-

-Sigh, Jeffro please, stop-

-My job is to be a great student and I am, what I do with my free time is my business... and I just created some free time, so if you would excuse me- Jeff said walking past him, Matt looked at everyone and stared at Randy, who couldn't hold the look, so Matt left.

Randy took all of them in his car, and they went to the ice cream parlor on the park. But Jeff seemed uncomfortable. Cody was delighted to have Randy hanging out with them again.

-So now we take my brother's leftovers? What is that reject doing here?- Randy looked at him angrily.

-Jeff, he's my boyfriend- Astrid said with her mouth full of ice cream.

-No, hes not, I am- Jeff stood up and kissed Astrid on the lips. -Oh, wow, I want whatever she's having, be right back- Jeff went to the cashier and the rest huddled up.

-Ok, are we addressing the fact that Jeff has lost his m nd?- Mickie said worried.

-Well, he's gonna loose some teeth when he comes back- Randy was so angry he punched the couch and teared it.

-We have to be patient with him, he just lost his father a couple months ago, he'll get better, plus, Randy, I think Matt would appreciate that you take care of his brother- Randy stood up angrily to Astrid's words.

-Who said I care whatever that idiot thinks or wants?! I knew hanging out with stupid kids was a mis-ake- he looked at Astrid who was actually confused. -Except for you, see you later woman- he gave her a kiss and left. Jeff came back and felt the tense air.

-Uy, what's going on? What happened to Randy?- he said eating his ice cream with his whole face.

-Ummm, I told him to accept the fact that you and I are together, and always will be- Astrid said with the fakest smile she could fashion. Cody gave Mickie a look as he took Jeff away to clean his face, so she can talk to Astrid.

-Are you out of your dang mind?!- Mickie said furious.

-Come on, Cody is not here, can we talk about what is really happening here?-

-I don't know what do you mean- Mickie seemed

nervous.

-Well, the fact that you like Jeff, like really like him-

-You can't say that! You know nothing-

-Chill, I won't tell Cody, but you deserve to explore that, believe me, Cody will understand-

-I don't think he will, plus, Jeff likes you-

-Jeff doesn't like me, that's the sadness talking, he misses his dad, and his dad was friends with mine... good friends, so he feels close to me, and thinks he likes me... but don't change the subject... you do like him, let me talk to Cody, I will make him understand-

Mickie was nervous, but she nodded. Cody came back with Jeff all cleaned up, Astrid stood up and took Cody away while Jeff sat with Mickie. Cody looked at them as they walked away, not comfortable with any of that.

-Astrid, what now?-

-You want to make up for what you did to Mickie?-

-OMG, more than anything in this life, but I can't tell her what I did, even though I just needed that to realize how much I love her and want to be with her-

-And how much you need to be my friend... yes, I get it, but what if I tell you you can make it up to

her without her knowing-

-I could kiss you!- he lifted her up. -But I won't because that would be gross, you're like my cool little sister- Cody said putting her down.

-MICKIE AND I ARE THE SAME AGE! Sigh, I won't argue about this again, point is, you need to let Mickie go on a date with Jeff, that way you'll get even- Cody looked at her thinking it was a joke, he even laughed a little.

-Letting her go... with a Hartford... on a date... with the same guy who just kissed you in front of Randy Omalley... HA! Asti, the stuff you say-

-I'm not joking, Mickie likes him- Cody boiled with anger. -Well, she thinks she likes him, she just needs one date to realize how much she loves you... you know like you needed months and to lose your virginity and stuff- Cody calmed down a bit, it was a small price to pay after what he had done, he took off and Astrid went back to their table.

-Astrid, where's Cody?- Mickie said nervous.

-Don't worry, he had some stuff to do, and so do I, but you can hang out with the new Jeff, I wish I could, please have fun!- Astrid left and Mickie and Jeff stared at each other.

-Is this a date?- Jeff said to break the awkward silence.

-I think so- Mickie said nervously.

-Well, I will marry Astrid, probably on a foreign country, under the stars... so this, you and me, could be weird, but I can tell you like me, that's fine, it's the Hartford charm- Jeff kissed her passionately... but none of them felt it. -You see, you're just attracted to my aura, can't blame you-

-Wow, thanks, I can't believe how cool you are about it... about everything... what happened to you?- Jeff turned sad for a moment but he shook it off.

-The day my father left I found out a case of him, I opened it and it was filled with jewels, you know, diamonds and stuff, so I immediately knew what his "business" were, right before he left he told me I would get everything I want in life, so until I get there I should just enjoy the ride, little did he know I took the jewels and gave them to the police, so he couldn't sell them... little did I know that he was sent to get those jewels and shouldn't show up without them- Jeff started to cry and Mickie hugged him. -I sent him to a certain death, it's my fault, when I realized it, I went to your father, since mine told me he was his friend once- Mickie was surprised she never knew about it. -I see he never told you, he told me my father was a filthy thief and he deserved to die, that's when I went to Mr. Callaway, and he helped me out, he took me to the police, then to the senate, and no one wanted to

get involved with international affairs, they didn't see a man struggling for his family, they only saw a thief, so we couldn't save my father, then Mr. Callaway offered my brother a job in the business if he finished his studies on the weekends. So Matt left everything to take care of me... my brother, the no-good-scum my father was so disappointed at... now he's my caregiver, cool, so I have to follow in his footsteps, I was his favorite, he said I had potential. See it like this, life got me here, and life will take me to my dream goal, so I'm just enjoying this nice piece of middle we're in-

Mickie looked at him perplexed as he smiled like he was telling her a sweet bedtime story. Jeff had always been a smart guy, studious, but as shy as he was he never spoke words like that, so deep, and changing to a rebel, it looked weird to hear such words from someone dressed like him and behaving like him. He stood up and offered her his hand. They walked to Mickie's house and Jeff kissed her on the porch.

-Date over, right?- Mickie said with a smile.
-Most amazing date I've had ever, thanks for listening-
-Thanks for letting me in, we should do this more often-

-I ain't kissing you again Jameson, so I hope you got a taste of that last one to remember-

-Ugh, I meant hang out, you're the worst Jeff-

Mickie laughed and went inside. Jeff left to his house. Mickie said goodnight to her father and ran to her bedroom to call Astrid. She told her the whole story of how Jeff gave up on being a shy little goody-two-shoes, to become a criminal with a big heart. But also about him telling her that they couldn't be together because he liked Astrid, and how none of them felt a thing after kissing.

New Gang Dynamics

Jeffrey... well, Jeff now, was a cahoot. Astrid was fascinated by his boldness and his carelessness while being the best student in every single class. She couldn't figure out when he could study when he was the whole time either in juvie or hanging out with them. A big test was coming up and they decided to meet at Cody's house to study.

-Ok, Jeff, tell us your secret!- said Astrid intrigued. Jeff was silent a long while, then he looked at her.
-Ok, I'll just say it, I'm definitely in love with you- he said as he shrugged. Cody fell on his back laughing. Astrid blushed.
-Jeff!!! I mean to study and know all this stuff-
-Oh, ok, I get it, look- Jeff got under the table.
-What are you looking for down there?- Astrid said between scared and giggly. Jeff popped his head out and closed his eyes.
-Oh, no, I need something first!- he got out and put a CD on Cody's stereo, it was a recording (illegal recording) of the teacher teaching, he then got back under the table and popped his head out. - Now we sleep, and we let the teacher teach- he

closed his eyes and slept there.

-Do I need to get under the table too?- said Astrid confused looking under the table for a little space.

-Only if you're cold too- Jeff said with his eyes closed. Astrid fell asleep there on the table, while Cody watched them be idiots. He wanted to laugh, but he didn't want to wake them up.

Cody got out of the room to call Mickie, her date with Jeff was a week ago, and she hasn't been able to talk to Cody directly, she felt so embarrassed, little did she know, Cody had a lot more to be embarrassed about.

-Mickie, dear, please, pick up, this is like the 25th message I leave in three days, you know I'm not like this, it's weird, I love you, you know I do, and I'm sure you love me, if you didn't you'd be with Jeff right now... unless you're not with him just because he likes Astrid. Come on Mickie Jameson, I'm freaking out here! I don't know what to do without you, if you don't love me anymore just face me and say it, but don't do...- Cody was interrupted by a beep.

-The mailbox capacity is full- said a voice on the phone. Cody stared at the phone.

-She hasn't heard any of my messages- he said with tears in his eyes.

-I have, I haven't deleted them though, I think I can use them against you when the time is right- Mickie said from behind him. Cody turned around so happy. He ran to her and lifted her up with a kiss. -I can't believe you were avoiding me- he said hugging her tight. Mickie looked at him embarrassed.

-Jeff and I kissed... twice... but it meant nothing- Cody smiled and kissed her. -Yup, nothing like that- they both smiled and kissed again. They entered Cody's room to find Astrid and Jeff spooning like cold babies under the table. Cody and Mickie stood at the door looking at them with tenderness, but it got old very quick and Cody slammed the door behind him.

-ALEXANDER HAMILTON WAS THE FIRST SECRETARY OF TREASURE!!!- said Jeff and Astrid at the same time, they looked at each other and Astrid smiled from ear to ear.

-I can't believe it actually worked- said Cody with his hand on his head.

-It did, Alexander Hamilton was a lawyer... and an economist... and he fought on the Battle of Yorktown in 1781! OMG I know history!!!- Astrid was really excited, History was the hardest for her, she hugged Jeff and kissed him, then realized what she just did and apologized.

-I told you that's how I study, sleeping is a waste of good time, so I use it to study. While you sleep your body shuts down to the minimal energy use, it's called Basal Metabolism, so it's actually more relaxed and receptive- Jeff said as he stretched. - BTW, you don't have to be embarrassed of kissing me, I love you too, and if it's because I already kissed your best friend, we're not weird about it, it didn't work between us- Astrid looked at Cody, seeing him hurt by Jeff and Mickie's kiss, and Jeff misinterpreted completely the situation. -OMG! I get it, I'm so sorry!- he walked up to Cody and kissed his lips. -There! now you all have kissed me, and no one has to be weird about my relationship with Astrid!-

-Oh no- Astrid said as she saw Cody get angry, but at the top of his anger... he burst out laughing.

-Wow Mickie, you must really love me, he's a great kisser- he said when he could calm down, Mickie stared at him in awe. Jeff looked at Mickie, and put on some imaginary sunglasses.

-I told you Mickie... the Hartford charm- Jeff said blowing a kiss to Mickie, to which she giggled.

Astrid, studied, and now also relaxed, went home. She got in and heard Shane fighting in the kitchen "Again his fight against my dad" she thought, but she entered the kitchen to an unusual scenario.

-You have to be dumb, or handicapped, or have some mental issue!!!- Shane yelled to Mike.
-I just said...-
-I know what you said, and I hate you forcing me to take Paul's side on all of this!-
-What is wrong with me taking Astrid on a trip?-
-EVERYTHING!!!- Shane said, grabbing Mike and shaking some sense into him. They both saw Astrid, and Shane released Mike.

-It's not what it looks like, princess- Shane said. Mike walked towards her and Shane got in the middle.
-Astrid, you would love to go on a little road trip with me back to Connecticut, right?-
-On... your bike?- Astrid said a little uncomfortable. -All the way to Connecticut? I know I was born there, and I loved to move here when Drew was taken away, so I have nothing to go there for... actually I'd be happy never to go back- Astrid said while walking back to go upstairs.

Astrid entered her room and heard some knocks on the window...Cody?...Randy?... well no, it was Jeff. She opened the window and smiled... between scared and really scared she was glad to see a friend.
-What are you doing here?- Astrid said while

helping him up the window.

-I wanted to see you... nice room- he said as he walked into her wide ass bedroom.

-Jeff, you've been here before, what do you need?-

-Oh, I see you're not in the mood, what's wrong with you?- he said jumping on the bed all gossipy.

-Mike and Shane are fighting because Mike wants to take me to Connecticut and...-

-And everyone told him he's crazy and he sucks, and his bike smells like a giant's feet's fungus!- Jeff said a little altered. -Sorry, continue- he rested his head on Astrid's lap and she stroke his multicolored hair to calm him down.

-Well, sorta, my dad and uncle said no, and even I said no, I don't want to go back to Connecticut-

-What happened there?- Jeff got up and caressed her cheek. He sat next to her and hugged her while she cried a little.

-I was born there, and the neighbors had a kid at the same time, his name was John and he was my best friend since we were born. We would be babysitted together, you know to save the neighbors some money, we got into the same daycare, because my parents didn't want to separate us, so they paid for him to go to the same daycare as me, my brother was already in preschool, and he would keep an eye on us-

-WAIT! You have a brother?!-

-It's a longer story, he's the prince of Scotland... that's why my family calls me princess, cause I used to get jealous of them calling him prince-

-Huh, that actually makes sense- Jeff sat in awe and kept listening.

-As I was saying... when we were 3 years old, a kid moved to town from Cleveland and became John's best friend, and one day at camp he became my boyfriend, and life was amazing!-

-So why do you hate Connecticut... it sounds like you had fun-

-My brother was taken to Scotland and my grandpa forced us to move and leave everything-

-Well, at least you have friends there!- Jeff said trying to cheer her up.

-No, I took John and his friend with me, it wasn't easy, but my parents saw me so crushed about my brother that they made it happen-

-THEN TELL THEM TO GO WITH YOU!!!- Jeff said desperate hearing this worsening story.

-John's parents died on a car accident- Astrid said ignoring Jeff's interruption. Jeff stood silent covering his mouth, he knows what that's like... sorta. -John was adopted by a nice family and his friend's dad got offered a great producer job back in Cleveland... so he left too. Everything great I had in Connecticut doesn't exist anymore, Connecticut just reminds me of all the happy things I've lost-

Jeff let out a tear and dried it almost immediately.
-But you don't have to go there, you have me now-
Jeff said as he kissed her softly on the lips. -And I
assure you even when everyone goes, I will always
be by your side- he said holding her hand.
-Jeff- Astrid chuckled. -Stop kissing me, I have a
boyfriend-
-I honestly don't care, what we have is stronger
than whatever you guys have, no pressure breaking
up, I know he can be a really tough one- Jeff said
as he looked out the window measuring his escape.
-You leaving already? Never told me what you
needed-
-On, true, you left these books at Cody's, not that
you be needing them anymore, I also brought you a
copy of the history recordings, I made copies at
Cody's because they wanted one, my method is da
bomb- he said as he jumped out the window
holding a rope.

Astrid smiled, she somehow knew that Jeff was a
friend she'll had forever and that it would be really
hard to keep him away. She went on the hallway
outside her room and she could still hear Shane and
Mike fighting downstairs. She ran into Paul's study.
Paul seemed really worried.

-Daddy, Shane and Mike are fighting- Astrid said

as she entered the study.

-Don't worry Asti, they're fighting over nothing, because there is no way in hell, that you go on that trip- he said without lifting his head for the papers.

-Daddy... are you ok?-

-I'm checking family stuff, I'm making sure our future is secured, you know how your grandfather gets, spending money and firing people, someone has to check on profit balance so we can survive- Astrid sat on his lap and held his head on her hands.

-But why you? Why not his actual son? Uncle Shane- Paul started laughing and crying. -What did I say? Isn't uncle Shane some kind of CEO like grandpa Vince?-

-HAHAHAHAHAHAHAHAHA noooo, Shane is our Chief of Ethics Officer, basically a high paid useless position, for him to sit and earn lots of money-

-But uncle Shane could help you either way-

-Uncle Shane should be in college... and where is he? Living out of his sister and his daddy while getting big checks monthly-

-I truly want to be like him when I grow up- Astrid said looking at the void. Paul shook her, laughing, to get her out of the trance.

-Thanks sweetie, I really needed to laugh a little-

-You know that's what I'm here for Daddy- Astrid

went sad for a second.

-What happened princess?-Paul said worried.

-I miss Drew-

-Don't we all, but you'll see him again, maybe at a funeral, or on Vince's next trip to Scotland, maybe he'll take you, I don't know, just know he's with his family and he's doing great over there, either way he will always be our prince and you will always be our princess, so don't you ever worry-

Astrid was happy again, she left Paul, now happier, with his papers and went out, it seemed like the two lovebirds downstairs stopped fighting, so she went down. Mike had left, and there was not a plate for him at the dinner table.

-Uncle Shane? What...-

-Mike won't be hanging out with you for a while, he's my friend, so he'll hang exclusively with me-Shane said handing Astrid a glass of wine (grape juice).

-I'm actually ok with that, I have a boyfriend now and having Mike on my back 24/7 was a little embarrassing- Astrid and Shane cheered and had an amazing dinner. Shane carried Astrid to her bed, she was exhausted, Paul was waiting to tuck her in and they all went to sleep.

The next morning Randy came to pick her up on his car, weirdly enough Jeff was on the back seat... oh oh.

-Astrid, my love- they both said at the same time. Randy turned around and Jeff laying on the back seat didn't seem worried at all.
-Jeff, what do you mean?- Randy said trying to calm down.
-Don't worry Rands, I respect your relationship while it last, just know that she won't be having YOUR children- he said looking at the sky through the sunroof.
-SHE'S HAVING WHO'S THEN?!- Randy, furious turned to Astrid. -ARE YOU...?- he said looking at her belly.
-OMG RANDY NOOO- Astrid was embarrassed and insulted. -I can't believe you even asked that!-

It was an awkward ride to school and when they got out Randy took Jeff by his shirt, threw him out of the car, and just like that, without saying a word, he started beating the crap out of him. Astrid had to pull them apart, Jeff ran away and Astrid took Randy by the tie like it was a dog leash, everyone saw them enter the school like that. Randy was Astrid's little pet. Randy was embarrassed, but deep down he felt he deserved it for beating up his best friend's baby brother.

-Do you understand why am I dragging you around with a leash?-
-No, I thought it was some weird fetish of yours, I'm just rolling with it- said Randy a little awkward. Astrid blushed and let him go.
-NO! You're...ew... no! It's not a fetish, it's because you're an animal and I have to keep you on a short leash! How was that a fet.... no, I don't want you to answer that- the bell rang right there saving her, she saw Mickie and ran to her, threw her arm over her shoulders and walked with her. Jeff didn't go to any of his classes that day, nor to the after class ice cream.

Checkpoint

It was almost the end of the year, a tough one for everyone involved.

a Randy lost his best and only friend, he lost his sister too, and his parents blamed him, because she was just "Trying to help him", so he grew colder and colder, not towards Astrid though, she managed to keep him just where she wants him.

a Cody saw his girlfriend choose someone else, the same way he did, and then come back to him, and it opened his eyes, "Butts come and go, but friendship is forever" so he found out that his only constant is Astrid and focused on her his complete attention, because even if he loved Mickie with all his heart, now he will never be sure of her feelings.

a Mickie, got closer with Jeff, even though there was no chemistry, she gained a confident, who loved Astrid... because nowadays everyone loves Astrid: Mike, Shane, Randy, Jeff, Cody. She almost wished she was her, but then again she would never, she knew that she couldn't trust Astrid, because, well, she was dumb and full of bad ideas... like asking Cody to let her go out with Jeff, losing his trust forever.

a Jeff, got into a delusional state, he learned to fear Randy, yet again, when it was only Astrid and him, he seemed to actually think they were together, and sent her weekly roses with Skittles. He got everyday more confident, hanging out with the wrong people for the right reasons, stealing for fun, then giving the stuff back, spending quality time in Juve, living life to the fullest. He never held something in, always acted the way he felt, and that gave him the peace most seek. But then again got him in jail... a lot.

a Mike grew more and more jealous everyday, he couldn't stand that Astrid had an older boyfriend, and that she wouldn't hang with him anymore. He realized he had strong feelings for her, feelings that if known by Shane will cost him his head. But Astrid didn't know about it, if she did she wouldn't look at him the same way ever again.

a Matt became the toughest caregiver ever. He left the immature life he was living on Randy's side and got a job while he finished school on saturday nights, he will graduate with Jeff probably at this pace, but it was fine by him, because he had money and a promise of a greater job when he finished. He wasn't that happy with Jeff's new delinquent ways, but he knew that behind his tough face there was a boy with a broken heart just like his, so he taught him how he used to bribe the police, and keep the authorities happy to keep jail time at minimum.

a Shane was living the life. He had an administrative job on his dad's company, which basically means that he's getting paid for doing absolutely nothing, but that money is saved since he's living out of her sister's money in her house. He fights with Paul every day over whatever, which he loves. He has his best friend technically living with them. His favorite niece, who idolizes him, is blooming into a strong, confident, young woman. Nothing goes wrong for Shane... ever!

a Paul, on the contrary, has his wife living on France. Paul has to raise his daughter by himself, and adding his baby brother in law and his brother in law's best friend, the two people who hate him the most in this world, are under his roof as well. Paul is definitely the one suffering the most here. But he has a beautiful, independent (most of the time) and confident young girl who loves him and needs him, and that makes him get up every morning with a smile.

The Godfather

Randy went to pick up Astrid like any other Tuesday morning. Astrid was running late, so he decided to go inside to see what happened.

-Who says you are invited in here?- said Mike blocking the door.
-Mr. Arlington, I recommend that you step out of my damn way!- Randy said angrily pushing Mike. Mike pushed him back and they were about to start a fight, when Shawn came out of the house. Randy shivered as he looked at him.
-Wow, Mr. Shawn! I'm sorry you had to see that, I'm a big fan- he said lowering his head with respect.
-Well I advise you get the hell out of this house, and I'll be taking my goddaughter to school today-
-Yes tell him Shawn- Mike said all cocky.
-You too Mike, you don't live here, and honestly, you got entrance here basically because I was away on business- Mike had to leave, embarrassed, just like Randy. Shawn came back inside to the sweetest tea party.

-It's weird that neither Randy nor Mike has shown

up to take me to school, but I'm glad you're back uncle Shawn-

-Ummm, they asked me politely if I could take you to school today and I gladly said yes-

-YOU'RE TAKING ME TO SCHOOL!!! You're an academy legend! People will die when they know you're my godfather!-

-I wouldn't say a legend- Shawn said trying not to brag. -But it's been a while since I haven't seen that future husband of yours-

-Uncle Shawn, that's disgusting, Cody and I are just friends-

-For now... just grab your bag-

Shawn, Paul's all time best friend, and Astrid's godfather. He came back from a 3 year trip to Paris as an ambassador for the company. He is as intimidating as a Grisly Bear and as sweet and nice as a Baby Panda. It just depends on which side you fall. Paul woke up and went downstairs as he felt Shawn. They saw each other and ran to each other, Paul lifting Shawn on a big hug.

-You son of a gun! I missed you!- said Paul almost crying.

-You beast! You're gonna crush me!- laughed Shawn.

-I thought you were not coming back since you

left with my wife-

-That sounds awful Hunter, I didn't "leave with your wife" We just went to the same place at the same time, but you know there's nothing between us-

-Well, it wouldn't be the first one we shared- Paul elbowed Shawn, to which Astrid stood disgusted.

-Uncle Shawn, can we go, you're gonna make me puke the croissant you made me-

-You made croissants?! How long have you been here?!-

-Well, I BROUGHT croissants, and I got here early in the morning, got in with my key and woke up Astrid to have a little French tea party before school-

-Mommy asked him to! So I would remember the ones she and I had all the time!- Astrid said excitedly hugging her father. Paul smiled and sent her on her way. Shawn smiled as she ran through the door and followed her to his car. Shane came down when they left.

-What was all that noise Paul?- he yawned.

-You're outnumbered scum, Shawn is back, so that means, your days in this house came to an end-

-Is my sister back too?- Shane said scared.

-Nope, she graduates in a couple weeks, but as soon as she's here you're out!-

Shawn strutted into school like he owned the place,

as related to the family as he is, he practically does. He went into the hall where his face was on a big plaque after he saved the Academy in what they call "The curtain call". Shawn was not only an Academy legend, he was a hero, everyone wanted to meet him, people stoop over each other to see him, and Astrid was loving it.

-You know Mr. Shawn?!- said the kids in awe.
-Well, he's my dad's best friend...- Astrid said with pride but was interrupted.
-...And I'm her Godfather as well!- Shawn said lifting her onto his shoulders, the crowd went wild, and Astrid was as popular as one could be.
-Hi, my name is Zack, from the school paper, tell us what brings you back Mr. Shawn?-
-First, take care of my little munchkin- he said putting Astrid down and ruffling her hair. -And second, I was offered to be the Academy's Principal- everyone went silent, no one could believe it, Astrid screamed and everyone followed her. Astrid knew that now she had control over absolutely everything... or so she thought.
-You're gonna be Principal?! This is the best day ever!-
-Yes, and my first command as acting Principal is sending you all to class-
-Wha...?-

-TO CLASS!!!- everyone ran away to their classrooms, but Astrid stayed.

-God-daddy, what's going on?-

-To be honest munchkin, they didn't ask me out to be Principal, your grandfather Vince fired the previous one and sent me here to run the Academy-

-Ugh, grandpa loves to fire people, but what about the school board?-

-We try to think that your grandfather is not the sole ruler of this school, but we all know he is, the board does whatever he says, or you think that Hartford could get a job without graduating just like that? The board was against it and Vince just moved his magic finger and got him an assistant something so he could provide for his family-

-Maybe he just feels guilty- Astrid said turning around.

-Guilty for what?-

-For killing Mr. Hartford- Astrid ran away, just to make Shawn chase her, she got into her classroom and sat there, and a few seconds later Shawn appeared on the door, not tired at all, as if he just materialized there.

Excuse me Mrs. Young, but Miss Callaway needs to go to my office- everyone looked at Astrid who had the biggest smile, she stood up all cocky and strutted to the door, Shawn was about to go outside when she ran and jumped him.

-You mean our office, God-daddy- Shawn smiled and he walked away with her clinging to his side, the way he saw it, Astrid was training her upper body strength. They went to the Principal's office to talk and Vince was standing there, he was weak and old, but he would NEVER show it. Astrid ran to him and hugged him.

-Shawn we need to talk- said Vince with a smile looking at his beautiful granddaughter. Shawn opened the door for him and Astrid stood outside.

Vince looked at Shawn intensely, he walked towards the desk's chair... Shawn's chair, and sat there like it was his.

-I want to thank you for being such a loyal employee, and for taking care of my family as I asked-

-I've told you Vince since Steph was a teenager, that spying on people is my passion-

-If I ever have to go, please don't leave her alone-

-She's never gonna be alone Vince, you have my word-

-I don't need your word, you and I are in all of this together, since I inherited the company, you've been there, by my side, since we were here in the

Academy, I remember you entered a year after I graduated and then the Curtain Call-

-That was as surprising for me as it was to the other guy- said Shawn, trying not to brag, again.

-You saved this Academy, which is the future of our company, and since, you've protected my family, risking yours, I don't need your word, I know you'll never fail me-

Vince got up and shook Shawn's hand. He got out of the office and Astrid was waiting out there on a chair, he said goodbye to her and hugged her, gave her a lollipop and left. Shawn ran outside to see if Astrid was still there, when he saw her, he grabbed her by the arm and looked everywhere checking for spies and pulled her into the office.

-What did you mean when you said Vince killed Mr. Hartford?- he said as they got in, locking the door, letting Astrid go and sitting with a serious face.

-Look, we all know we run this city, it's true, we left Connecticut because there wasn't anything else to own there. Fact: Mr. Hartford was my dad's friend, so he knew grandpa. Fact: Mrs. Hartford died and left them with a horrible debt, probably to my grandpa. Fact: He stole from Mickie's dad who was his best friend but my grandpa's long life foe, he was also stealing from my dad. Fact: Mr. Hartford died doing some business related to diamonds overseas. Fact: My Grandpa knows everyone who is capable of that level of rich. You just have to connect the dots, he couldn't keep stealing from his friends so he tried to pay my grandpa's debt by negotiating diamonds for him overseas but Jeff took the diamonds to the police, and he went to make an illegal negotiation without them and they asked my grandpa to have him killed, for stealing the diamonds, which Jeff did- Shawn was shocked by the coldness of his little munchkin, but even more by all the sense she was making right there.

-Have you shared these thoughts with anyone else?-

-No! I didn't believe them until you just said that, OMG, my grandpa killed Jeff's dad, I'm responsible for Jeff's transformation! Although I kinda like him better like this- aaaaand she was back.

-Calm down sweetie, you're not responsible in any way, and you don't know if that's what happened, I got you something to take your mind off of all of this-

-I like that, what is it?- she said forgetting the previous conversation.

-How do you like being the first freshman who gets to plan the senior's prom?-

Astrid's eyes sparkled, she obviously loved the idea,

she get to decide for Randy's prom and she knew exactly what the theme would be...

-THE FUTURE!!!- Astrid said banging the table at the Prom committee meeting.

-Miss Callaway we...-

-Call me Astrid- she said leaning on her chair and putting her feet on the table.

-Ok, Astrid, we were thinking on something more thoughtful and sweet... not robots and lasers- said the student president a little intimidated by Vince's granddaughter.

-Oh no, but the future is not all robots and lasers- Astrid stood up very inspired and convincing. -The future is what the seniors are facing now, yeah, I know the future seems the same for everyone, you graduate from here you come to work for me, but many people will choose other companies, even other careers. I know a few who are just here because their parents want them to... right Dwayne?- Astrid squinted at the student president with a smile, he blushed and stuttered a bit.

-I... I... I... don't know what you're talking about-

-I'm sorry, did you have a better idea Dwayne?-

-I thought we could...- Astrid cut him off abruptly.

-It doesn't matter what your idea is! We're doing The Future! Show of hands please!- Astrid was raising her hand alone... but she didn't care. -Done!

I'll go inform the Principal-

Astrid skipped to Shawn's office but found Randy on the hallway.

-Whatever you're doing to my prom, please don't, it's... it's the only senior prom I have and this hasn't been a good year, except for you- Astrid looked at him in the eye and moved closer, Randy swept her off her feet and kissed her passionately.
-Everything I do, I do it for you Randy Pandy- Astrid said a little dazed. Shawn showed up out of nowhere right behind them.
-Is this proper behavior for school halls Mr. Omalley-
-HOLY SH.... I'm sorry Mr. Shawn, I don't know what got into me- said Randy really scared.
-I think that was my tongue sir!- Astrid was actually having fun, Shawn looked at her and laughed, Randy tried to laugh but Shawn looked at him and he stopped. Shawn ruffled Astrid's hair and Randy ran to his class.
-You were coming to see me? How did it go with the student council?-
-It's funny to see Randy scared for a change- she said not paying attention to any of what Shawn was saying. -Let's go to my office, I have to talk to you- she said grabbing Shawn by the shirt all bossy.

The Senior Prom

Finally Astrid's prom was here. Well... Randy's prom. Everything was head-on Astrid's plan, she had the gym decorated with lasers, and futuristic chairs and tables, they had a punch robot which dispenses fruit punch like a cool juice butler. The ceiling had green and pink clouds and was full of stars like the space. There were panels all around with pictures of the seniors doing stuff related to the career they were more inclined to. Despite everything the council said, it was beautiful, and thoughtful, and actually fun, but she had one last surprise.

-I'm really glad you're here with me, honestly all I wanted tonight was to dance with you... and for the school not to burn to the ground- said Randy as he and Astrid danced a slow song.
-Are you sure that is all you want?- Astrid whispered in his ear, he lowered his head and nodded a little sad.
-Well, then I guess you'll be disappointed-
-Are you going to burn the school?- he said with a smile. Astrid laughed and he kissed her forehead. When the song ended Astrid went up to the stage.

-What's up my people from the future!!!- Astrid yelled and it was well received, even Randy yelled back. -The night is not over yet! We have been talking a lot about the future tonight, but there's one person you all know and love who has actually lived it- everyone looked at each other confused but Randy's eyes discreetly sparkled. -Give it up for currently employed, Matt Hartford!!!- Matt came out, all cute and dressed up, Randy almost cried, but that wasn't him, not anymore, he resisted being happy, and even more when he saw who was Matt's date.

-No effing way!- Randy crushed his punch cup and walked angrily towards Matt.
-Randy, it's been a while dude- Matt said offering his hand but Randy just looked at it and didn't shake it. -Ooookay, I would like you to meet Selena, we've been seeing each other for a little while now- Randy looked at him as if he was joking, Matt was the only person who actually knew his sister, but Matt looked at Astrid who was walking towards them just as angry as Randy.
-No effing way!- Astrid said looking at them. -How could you?! This was my moment to be a cool hero! Can't you go ruin it for someone else?! I thought you were in Paris!-
-Yes, I came back because my Matty had to go to

his prom and I wouldn't send him alone- Selena said rubbing noses with Matt. Randy was about to puke, his ex best friend and his older sister. Astrid, as the event coordinator, got her out, Matt understood and stayed, Selena was not so happy about that, but Matt only wanted to enjoy his prom with his friends, even if Randy wouldn't talk to him and if his girl wasn't with him.

-You should go talk to him, tell him how you feel- said Mickie when she sat next to Randy. Randy stood up and picked up Mickie from the ground. Mickie blushed embarrassed.
-What are you doing here? You're just a freshman-
-I came with Cody, Astrid invited us- she said nervous.
-I can't, people will look at me weird, my mom already thought Matt and I were seeing each other-
-Because you guys have one of those friendships that people will kill for, that's why you have to fight for it-
-But I will look weak- Randy complained.
-How do you think you look when Astrid pinches your cheeks and calls you Randy Pandy?-
-Hot- Randy lifted an eyebrow and looked at her.
-Ok, that's true- Mickie blushed a second and looked away.

-But with a guy is different, I'm not gay, nothing against it, but I'm just not-

-But this is your chance to fix things!-

-You're right, it is, I might never get another one-
Randy put her down, and walked away decided, Mickie felt so proud. Matt met him in the middle of the dance floor and people started to whisper.

-Bro, how's it going?- Matt said with a big smile. Randy lowered his head for a second and looked up to him with a smirk and a pretentious pose.

-Well how's it going, loser? How do you dare to show up here after they kicked you out?- Everyone laughed, Matt was shocked.

-Randy, you know that's not what happened?-

-What happened then, you couldn't bare seeing your delinquent father dead and flunked everything? Let me just tell you, your little brother is on the same path! And you can't get it out!- Matt got really angry and remembered Randy's secret.

-That's not what your sister said last night!- the crowd went silent, Randy choked, he looked at Astrid but she was silent as well, Matt couldn't do that to him. -Neither your mom, nor your aunts, yes, I banged your whole family!- Randy breathed and the crowed oooh-ed back.

-Well you are just another uneducated reject, and you won't last a year on that pity job your brother's friend got you, because we all know you wouldn't have gotten it if it wasn't for Astrid-

-Well, that says a lot of you, because you're banging her and she hasn't gotten you a job yet... ohhh that's right, you're not even banging her, she wouldn't even let you go to second base!- Matt dropped the mic and left, he didn't want to "prom" anymore, he was passed all that, he needed that last immature gesture, but Randy knew what Matt did when he saved his secret, and secretly he would thank him for it.

-Nothing to see here, let the party continue!- to Randy's words the DJ turned the music up and everyone continued dancing.

-I saw you talking to Randy right before, what was that?- Astrid said really concerned.

-I just told him he should talk to Matt and told him that this was his only chance, he was really concerned about people mistaking their bromance for actual romance, ugh, he's a brute Astrid, he's an ogre with no heart!-

-Mickie, that's the guy you were drooling for like a year ago-

-I didn't know him then, I didn't know what he was capable of-

-What are you two hotties talking about?- Cody approached the girls with some slick dance moves.

-Randy, as always- Astrid said very vaguely while she searched for Randy through the crowd. -Have you seen him?-

-I think he went outside- Cody said grabbing Mickie and spinning her around. Astrid went out and saw Randy kicking the trash cans with rage, he seemed furious, but sad, she got closer and saw him almost cry, but it could have been sweat.

-Randy, are you oka...-

-OF COURSE I'M NOT!!!- he said kicking another can.

-Talk to me- Astrid sat on the side walk. Randy calmed a bit and sat next to her.

-Didn't you see me in there? That wasn't me, and you know it, I love Matt, he's my best friend, but the things he told me-

-Ugh, and showing up with that stupid bitch-

-Umm, yeah, I know what that girl did to you, that shocked me too, to see them together, but what I mean is I should've been more brave and reconcile with him instead of trying to humiliate him, his father liked me more than he did Matt...- Randy smiled at the ground. -He would've been very disappointed to hear me say those things- Astrid put her hand on his cheek. -But that little Jeffrey sucks, that I actually meant, he's going down a dark path- Astrid laughed and pushed him away with the same hand that rested on his cheek, he took her hand and they kissed. And the world seemed right for that night.

They went back inside and danced with Mickie and Cody, they enjoyed a prom that was to talk for the ages. When it all went down Randy offered to take Mickie home to apologize to her, Astrid let him and went home with Cody.

-What happened to your boyfriend today? He roasted Matt like a pig!-
-I know, he was wrong, he knows it, but there's no going back now, he'll have to live with that regret, he's gonna need a lot of love now-
-Tons of love, got it- Cody closed the door in the car and went inside with her.
-Miss Callaway, always a pleasure to see you- said Max while he took her purse.
-Thanks Max! You're the coolest! sometimes I wish I had a butler at home, and then I realize no one could compare to you!- she said leaning on him batting her eyelashes, to which Max didn't even move.
-Thanks Miss Callaway, I'm flattered- he left to the kitchen to get the kids some snacks.

The perfect snacks at the perfect sleepover with

the perfect friend, after the perfect prom with the perfect guy, makes the perfect night. But everything goes great for Astrid... doesn't it?.

The Funeral

The time came when Astrid's mom had to come back, an awful day for some and an amazing day for others. Astrid's parents love story was an unconventional one. Astrid's mom was engaged to a guy named Test, who was best friends with her, and also with Shane and Mike, the whole family was ready to bring Test in, but the day of the wedding, Astrid's dad showed up with a video of them getting married in Vegas on a drive-through chapel. They all got really angry and Astrid's mom cried her eyes out, but her dad forced her to move with her husband. She secretly kept on seeing Test, until a year after wedding when he died mysteriously. She then learned to love her husband and a year later Astrid was born.

-I'm glad I got to see you before school, Astrid, I'm so sorry I missed your first year at the academy, but I got all your letters- said Stephanie walking into Astrid's room.
-Mom, you're back!- Astrid jumped out of bed and hugged her, she then realized that her uncle had to go. -No!-

-Wow, you have to decide- she laughed.

-Mom, if you're back it means that uncle Shane is leaving-

-You know I love my baby brother with every inch of my body-

-Ok, gross-

-But I just can't stand him fighting your father, and flooding my head with conspiracy theories about you know who- Astrid understood and hugged her mom excited again.

-Well, I'm glad you're here, there is so much to talk about! I have a boyfriend! I have a criminal friend! I am as popular as it can be! UNCLE SHAWN IS MY PRINCIPAL!!!- Astrid was so excited she woke up her uncle Shane and her father, they both ran to her room, stepping on each other to reach her first... but when they crossed the door...

-STEPHANIE!!!!- Paul ran to her and lifted her with a kiss, spinning her around. She laughed and kissed him.

-Hunter, I missed you so much!- she said with tears in her eyes, then she looked at Shane... and did almost the same.

-SHANO!!!!- Stephanie ran to him and lifted him, spinning him around, Shane was really uncomfortable and embarrassed but he smiled softly. -The most beautiful baby brother in the

world!-
-I'm not a baby, Steph! I'm an adult now, I'm 24!-
-Then why am I still paying for your phone and Hunter still picks you up at soccer practice?- she said putting him down and ruffling his hair.
-Because I'm smart...- he dusted himself off. -And I like soccer- they laughed but Paul couldn't contain himself.
-Ok, Shane, it's time to be smart somewhere else!- they all looked at him. -What? Come on, everyone was thinking about it, I just expressed it- Astrid looked at her uncle and hugged him, he knelt and looked at her in the eye.
-I'll come visit you, I swear, I'll be back for your 19th birthday, one day I told you I would visit every five years, and you just got three whole years of uncle Shane, I'll be gone for a while, but you'll see me again- Shane hugged her and they both cried. -On the meantime just call your father Paul whenever you want to feel me close... you know he hates it- Astrid nodded and hugged him, then his phone rang.

-Daddy?!... No, I wasn't crying... WHAT?! Why?... that's insane even for you... I'm sorry Daddy I didn't mean that... yes, she just got back... sure, bye Daddy. Steph, Daddy wants to talk to you- Shane handed his phone to Steph.

-What?... Ok... When?... Ok... I love you too- Steph hung up and walked out without saying a thing, very serious. Paul and Astrid looked at Shane for answers.

-Daddy said he wants us to organize a funeral?-

-Is grandma okay?!- Astrid said with tears.

-Yeah, she's fine, it's for... him, he wants us to organize his funeral now so he can enjoy it, the doctors gave him max 3 years, so he wants to see what his funeral would be like... I guess he will lay on a coffin and watch the people who care about him cry their eyes out for no reason-

Shane was right, it was insane even for a dying rich old man, but he wanted to be prepared, so it wasn't just the funeral, he had his will checked out, all his belongings and physical money will be sorted now, so whenever he dies no one has to do anything for him. Astrid had to be sad, but she couldn't because her mother had the perfect job for her... find her brother. She made like a hundred phone calls and finally reached her brother's parents.

-Hi... Mr. McLane?... Good... I'm Astrid Callaway, Stephanie Brooks' daughter, I'm calling to inform you my grandpa Vince died and we're having his funeral tomorrow afternoon, it would mean a lot to him if you could come... I mean to us, it would mean a lot to us if you could come, and bring Drew!... thanks, hope to see you here-

Astrid was excited to see her brother again, he wasn't actually her brother but they grew up together as siblings until his parents took him back. Mr. McLane, was Vince's best friend so he called Vince directly and he informed the plan, he wouldn't let Drew go through the news of losing his godfather without knowing the whole truth. Paul and Astrid went for them to the airport.

-ASTI!-
-DREW!- they ran to each other and looked intensely into each others eyes. They hugged, but Drew's mom came and pulled them apart.
-Andrew, we're at the airport, you can't have those public displays of affection, that's not what the royals do-
-Sorry mom- Drew lowered his head, he didn't want to be a prince, he just wanted to be a kid, like the days when he lived with the Callaways.
-Astrid! you can't have those displays either, that's not what the Callaways do!- said Paul mocking the McLanes.
-I'm sorry Daddy, the Callaways make a much bigger deal!- Astrid jumped on him and kissed his head all over while Paul laughed, Drew smiled and

wanted to join, but his dad grabbed his shoulder and moved his head from side to side. Paul left them in their hotel and he begged to let Drew stay with them for the night but they said no, Drew had royal homework from the royal school that couldn't wait. Astrid went back home defeated, but glad to at least have seen her brother again.

They rounded up the funeral, it was a beautiful service, all of Astrid's friends were there with their parents... well except for Jeff, he was there with Matt. And she got to sit next to her brother Drew, with all the sadness of realizing her favorite grandpa just had a few years to live, she was ecstatic to spend time with her brother, they spent the whole service sharing laughs and looks, they went back to being kids, but what easy comes easy goes, and the funeral ended, Vince jumped out of the coffin in the end, scaring to death everyone who didn't know it was a pretend funeral, and without any time to lose the McLanes left the country that same night and went back to Scotland.

A New Year

The new year started! Astrid, Mickie and Jeff were now sophomores, and Cody was a Senior... surprisingly Randy was still a senior as well, he said he was willing to wait because Astrid can not be left alone to her own judgment. And he was sorta right.

That year, a boy got into the Academy. A shy kid, who immediately connected with Cody, a beautiful guy that immediately got in Randy's head, and a gorgeous hair that carved his way into Astrid's heart, no other than: Theodore Arlington Jr., Mike's younger brother, although if it wasn't for the last name, no one would know, because they were completely different. Mike moved to Connecticut with Shane after the funeral, even thought they don't live in the same house, they live right next to each other. So Ted was the only Arlington in town (well except for his parents and his baby brother Brett, of course). Cody, Mickie and Astrid were having a picnic at the Academy's picnic ground, but none of the girls were on the mood to eat anything.

-Guys, did you see the new kid? He's an Arlington- said Astrid fixing her hair on a spoon.

-Yes, he is, is he gonna be as creepy as his brother?- said Mickie doing the same.

-No one is ever gonna be as creepy as his brother-

-Did I miss something? I thought you two were the co-presidents of the Mike Arlington Fan Club- Cody said with his mouth full, pointing at them with his fork.

-Ugh, Don't you know what he did over the summer?- Mickie said disgusted.

-No, what happened?-

-I'll tell him Mix, after all, I'm the one damaged for life- Astrid got all serious, Cody started to worry. - When last year ended we went all camping for the summer, it was right after my grandpa's funeral. And let's be straight forward, Mike was flirting with me, and it was disgusting, and I confronted him, and he didn't deny it, which is even worse, he asked me to be his girlfriend, which was idiotic because first I'm with Randy and second he is TEN YEARS OLDER!!!-

Cody tried to look serious, but he couldn't and he burst out laughing.

-I'm honestly surprised he didn't do it sooner- Cody said calming down.

-What do you mean, you sick pervert?- Astrid said pushing him.

-I mean... he made you lay on top of him in your couch, he picked you up and brought you to school everyday when any of us could've taken you, or your father, oh right and he held hands with you whenever he got the chance- Cody said as if everything was too obvious.

-Now that you mention it, we should've known by the constant jealousy towards Randy- Mickie said realizing everything. Cody started laughing again. Astrid felt a little offended. Cody wrapped his arms around her and kissed her head.

-Your only flaw is being really really dumb- Mickie looked at him and he got her into a group hug. -You two need to open your eyes more, lucky for you I'll always be here to defend you!- he said saving his butt, he has grown to fear Mickie, she could leave him on a heartbeat.

-Hey Ted! Over here!- Cody shout out to Ted who was going to sit by himself. -He reminds me of the old Jeff, remember that?- Mickie nodded excited, Astrid couldn't help it and left just as Ted was approaching.

-I'm done! Gotta go to the Principal's office-

Astrid ran to Shawn's office and locked the door.

Shawn was early and saw her scared and just couldn't help but wonder.

-Astrid, are you ok? What are you running from?-

-I don't know, I honestly don't- Astrid sat on his desk. -The first day is always tough uncle Shawn, and now, seeing everybody, new people, it's overwhelming, I haven't seen my boyfriend since the funeral, and I miss him, all I know is he didn't graduate to keep an eye on me-

-I'm definitely eliminating pre-class breakfast, it makes no sense and it's a waste of money, I mean, you can have breakfast at home and stop over stressing-

-That's absolutely not the point... at all, what about the people that has no money for breakfast-

-I'm sorry to say it like this, but they just can't afford this school, with the exception of the only scholarship we ever granted, but even the Hartfords have money for breakfast-

-Fine, what about the people who live far and have to get their kids here early, and have no TIME for breakfast-

-Well...- Shawn thought it for a second. -Well then they will be the ones fit and ready for battle, you have to admit that as much as there are people who need it, there are some that eat both here and at home like...-

-Dwayne's twin cousins- they said at the same

time.

Astrid looked at him funny, but they both laughed. She hugged him and he sent her on her way to class. She was in every single class with Ted, but she avoided him at every cost. She secretly followed him through the halls just to watch him be bullied... THAT she couldn't bare.

-Hey you, bully someone your own size!- she shouted to the giant bully, he turned around... it was Randy... with short hair!!!! He was almost bald! Astrid tried to hide it but she started crying. He approached her to kiss her, but she pushed him away. -I don't know you, you're dead to me!-
-Let me explain- Randy said a bit annoyed by her drama.
-There is nothing to explain Randall, if you NEED to cut your hair, you better cut your head off!!- Astrid ran away and Randy wanted to chase after her but heard the whispering behind.
-Yeah, whatever, a thousand where that came from- his gang high-fived each other and he sadly joined them and kept picking on Ted. Ted let them just to feel part of something.

-Hey yo Cody, What's up?- Cody turned around to say hi but was shocked out of his socks when he saw him.

-Man, what happened to your head? uff, you can kiss your relationship with Astrid goodbye-

-What is it with her and hair anyways?-

-A think a witch told her in a dream that she would die inside if she cut just one lock of her hair... and got traumatized, because according to her it was 'more than a dream" I think you look bad ass, not that it matters- Cody fist bumped him and left, he had to find Astrid, and saw her sitting alone in her empty classroom.

-Hey, is this algebra?-Cody said pretending he was lost.

-No, it's ring measurement class... are you getting married?-

-Maybe one day, in a cool church, with Mickie, but not today no... You know that's not what this class is about, right?- Astrid shrugged. -I saw Randy- Astrid ran to him crying. -I imagine you broke up with him-

-DID YOU SEE HIS HAIRCUT?!-

-I did, it was awful, but hey, he didn't die-

-Didn't he? Have you seen him lately? He was a bully before, but a bully with a heart, with a code, now he's a hairless empty shell of a man- Astrid fainted into Cody's arms dramatically and he just laughed.

-You like Ted, Randy's hair was an excuse, and when he finds out he will just kill Ted, no biggie- Cody was right, Astrid realized that and promised to avoid Ted at all cost. Later that day, it was the last class and the Academy's speaker were open to an announce.

-Hello Academy, this is your Principal Shawn speaking, I'm announcing a little change of plans in our curriculum. Effective in two months, sophomores, juniors and seniors who'd like to work in the business need a 100 hours of supervised internship at one of our local developmental facilities, so you get the taste of the business before graduating.
-Hi Principal Shawn, can we talk?-
-Mr. Omalley I was... nothing, of course we can talk, is this about Astrid?- Shawn said discreetly pointing the microphone to him.
-Yes, it's about her, she broke up with me, and everything I did to stay was to be with her, so I wanted to know if I could graduate-
-Well, I'm afraid now you need your 100 hours of internship-
-I grew up on developmental, I know the business, plus you said effective in two months-
-The school year has already started and you enrolled as a senior, I can't give you a preferential

treatment just because-

-You know my father, even my grandfather, they're friends with the Brooks, I was your goddaughter's boyfriend, please please Mr. Shawn, get me out of here-

-D d you say please?-

-Well, umm, YES! Pretty please Mr. Shawn- Randy knelt before him and he grabbed the mic.

-You heard it here first folks, Randy Omalley begging for his life, just not to see the little girl who broke up with him- Shawn close the microphone and Randy stood up in shock, a tear ran through his cheek and he ran out.

The next week was hell for Randy, so he stuck to what he did best. Beat the crap out of people, specially Ted. That somehow gave Ted a name, because even though Randy bullied him, he had earned a place in his crew. After a week of fighting, Shawn gave Randy what he wanted, he graduated but had to go for training at their main developmental in two months when the other interns start as well.

1 month later

-Wow, who would've thought life could be so interesting in high school?- Astrid said to Mickie *as they were going out of class.*

-Yes, last month Randy graduated, and we start in developmental in three weeks! You should write a Diary, that should be amazing-

-Ha ha ha, I wouldn't even know how to start-

-I don't know, just write Dear Diary and write what happens, it's so liberating to tell someone everything, even the things you can't tell anyone-

-Uy, I have a few of those- Astrid and Mickie laughed when Cody approached them.

-Hello, ma ladies, wanna come with me for ice cream at the park?-

-No, sorry, uncle Shawn wouldn't let me-

-I fix that- Cody said as he saw Shawn coming out.

-My dear Mr. Principal, hope your day's going as great as mine became when I saw you come out just now- Astrid and Mickie looked at each other and chuckled softly while Cody bowed. -I was wondering if I could take young Astrid for ice cream at the park, I promise to return her home early in one piece and homework done-

-Anything for you little Cody, and you can return her late if you want to- Shawn said with a wink... Cody tried not to barf and nodded with an awkward smile.

The three of them went to the park and had way too much ice cream, they lied on the grass cloud gazing.

-Guys, I miss Jeff- Astrid said.
-Randy forbid him to hang with you because he still thinks that you two have something- said Cody turning to face them.
-I'm honestly more worried about when is Astrid going out with Ted- Mickie said with a smirk while watching the clouds.
-Oh yeah, we've talked about you, and he definitely thinks you are not ugly- Cody went back to look at the cloud, leaving Astrid a little anxious.
-Wow, that's vague, thanks-
-He just needs a push, ok, look, in three weeks I'm having a party at my uncle's club to celebrate the beginning of our internships, I'll invite Ted and you two could talk there without Randy's people listening and lurking in the halls-
-That sounds like a plan! He's gonna be our New Buddy!- Astrid sat up excited.
-Umm, your New Buddy, I'm kinda best friends with him and of course he's met Mickie plenty of times-
-Well, My New Buddy! This will be exciting!-

This story continues in
Astrid's Diary

Lightning Source UK Ltd.
Milton Keynes UK
UKHW051040020421
381418UK00006B/65